VARIETY PACK: READERS' CHOICE

BIG IDEAS: LOW INTERMEDIATE

ALICE SAVAGE

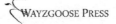

WAYZGOOSE PRESS

CONTENTS

INTRODUCTION

When you read something, like an article or story, you have a conversation. The writer shares information, experiences, and ideas – but you, the reader, have your own ideas. When you read, you compare your ideas with the writer's ideas. Then you think. Do you agree with the writer? Can you use the information to be healthier or more successful in your job, for example? Does the writer understands your life? Or do you learn about someone with a different life?

Big Ideas can start interesting conversations between readers and writers, but also between readers and other readers. How do you become a millionaire? Will humans ever travel to another world? Is it good or bad to talk to strangers? There is no right or wrong answer to these questions, but when you think about them, you learn language and information together.

There are also many other reasons for reading *Big Ideas*. The topics are important to modern life. Our readers report seeing similar topics on tests or in newspapers, magazines, and websites. People talk about these topics at school and at work. The easy-reader approach helps you explore these topics without spending hours with a dictionary or figuring out idioms.

Big Ideas also helps you learn English. Most of the words in this book are "high-frequency words." These words appear again and again in speaking and writing. However, they sometimes change their meaning when they appear with different words. For example, you know the word *up*. But it has different meanings in phrases like **up** *the road*, *look* **up** *the word in the dictionary*, *call* **up** *a friend*, and **up** *in the sky*.

To learn the different meanings of high frequency shadow words, read a lot. When you read, you see the words in different combinations, and you learn the meanings. This can happen naturally, but it will happen faster if you pay attention to words in groups, such as such as *stay awake* and *stay away*. When you notice and learn these word combinations, you can learn the different meanings.

Vocabulary connects to grammar, and grammar connects to sentences. In order to give you a positive reading experience, this book has easy-to-read sentences. We use grammar from low intermediate levels, and we reduce synonyms and idioms. Our goal is to keep the big ideas, but present them in language that is easy to understand.

We hope you will use this *Big Ideas* book in many ways. You can read the ebook on your phone or in a book, or read the paperback version. You can read at home, in class, or a on a bus or train. You can use the ideas and language to have a discussion with your English class or a conversation with a friend. You can use the reflection questions for writing or just for thinking. Our main goal is to provide interesting ideas so you can have something to talk about in English.

SUPPLEMENTARY MATERIALS

For *Big Ideas* downloadable learning tools for students and teachers, go to

http://wayzgoosepress.com/books/readers-choicevariety-pack-big-ideas-intermediate/

I

SUCCESS STORIES

It is hard to predict success. Business people want to sell popular products and services. Most try to improve products that are already on the market. This is safe because people know about these products.

However, other business people try something different. They do not listen when people tell them their idea will not work. They believe in themselves. Not all of these people succeed, but some of them do. Sometimes they become very successful, and they surprise everyone. Then their idea seems obvious, and people say, "Why didn't I think of that?"

THE KING OF K-POP

I n 2012, the Korean musician Psy had a hit song. The song was "Gangnam Style," and people heard it all over the world. The video got two billion views on the Internet. It was the most popular music video in the history of YouTube.

Psy's success was a surprise in the West. Many people expected the next top hit song to come from a Latin American country, England, or the United States. Music producers in these places have a lot of experience. They find new musicians and support their careers. There are concerts and a lot of publicity. However, business people cannot always discover a new *style* of musical artist.

In fact, Pay surprised many Korean music producers. They controlled Korean popular music (K-pop). Important music companies like SM were making millions of dollars by supporting serious and romantic bands. They gathered attractive young singers and dancers. They gave them lessons, and they made careful decisions about their look, their songs, and their lives. This way of creating new music worked well for them, and they did not think about changing.

Psy was different. He traveled to the United States as a young man. He started university, but then he quit. He wanted to focus on his own style of music. Psy's goal was to make people laugh and dance. He was not thin, serious, or attractive like other K-Pop stars. This was not the usual way to be successful.

Success did come, however. Psy uploaded some songs on the Internet, and they became popular. He could work as a musician, and he was able to make his own decisions. A producer liked his style and supported him.

His hit song, "Gangnam Style," tells the story of Gangnam, a rich neighborhood in Seoul, Korea. People go there to feel rich. They walk through the shops and buy expensive coffee. Psy decided to have a little fun. He wanted people to laugh at the Gangnam shoppers. He created a crazy video about a man trying to have Gangnam style. The man wants to attract a Gangnam girl, but he is a little silly. To make it light and fun, Psy added a funny dance. But the dancers were not sexy. They looked like they were riding a horse.

Koreans loved it, but so did the rest of the world. They liked the cheerful music. They learned the horse-riding dance. They also understood the message about money. Most people have mixed feelings about money. On one hand, it is nice to be rich and beautiful. On the other hand, sometimes people try to look rich, but they fail. They only look funny. Psy put all those feelings into a light musical experience.

Psy's success has been good for Korea. Now the world is watching the Korean music business. They are enjoying other Korean pop songs, and now more bands are having fun with their own style. However, there is also a lesson for musicians. Sometimes it is good to change music. Psy became an international superstar because he was different. He learned to tell a Korean story, but his Korean story was also a human story.

REFLECTION

1. What lesson can you learn from Psy's success story?
2. Can you describe another musician who changed music?

SARAH BLAKELY'S UNDERWEAR

S arah Blakely was always good at selling things. She sold office equipment for a time, but she wanted something more. Then she had an idea. She worked hard, and the idea became a business. Now Blakely is a billionaire. This is her story.

The idea started with a party. Blakely wanted to wear white pants, but she did not like the fit. She needed better underwear, so she designed her own. The underwear made clothes look better. She decided to call her product Spanx.

Blakely needed a factory to make the underwear, so she talked to different people in the underwear business. People laughed at her idea. Her design was not traditional. Clothing factories made underwear the same way in the same sizes, and they did not see the need for change. Blakely thought about them. They were men, and they did not understand.

Finally, one factory owner called her back. He said, "I will make your underwear." She asked him why, and he said, "Because I have daughters, and they like your idea."

Next, Blakely needed stores. She called a big, important

clothing store, and she asked for a meeting. She flew to Texas to meet the buyer. Blakely was a young woman with no money. She had a simple red backpack. It was her lucky backpack. Inside, she had an example of Spanx in a plastic bag.

When Blakely arrived, she spoke with a well-dressed woman. Blakely believed in herself, but she was also worried. The woman was not paying attention. Finally, Blakely said, "Come to the bathroom with me." The woman was surprised, but she followed Blakely into the bathroom. Blakely modeled the difference with her own clothes. With the special underwear, her clothes fit beautifully.

The woman understood. She agreed to put Spanx in seven stores. Sarah was happy, but she did not relax. She wanted women to know about the product. She went home and called her friends. She sent them money, and she asked them to go to stores and buy Spanx. She also set up tables in stores and talked to customers.

Next Blakely worked on the design. She made different shapes because women's bodies are different. Blakely also thought a lot about the package design. She used bright colors, and she did not use photography. Her mother was an artist, and she made designs for the package.

All this happened in Blakely's apartment. Her friends helped, but she did almost everything by herself. For example, she did not spend money on advertising. Instead, she called important people and made connections with them. Her efforts led to opportunities. Blakely went on television and talked about Spanx. Women learned more about the product, and sales increased. Blakely did almost everything herself, and she stayed in control of the company. Ten years later, Spanx was a billion-dollar business, and Sarah Blakely was famous.

Blakely's story did not end there. After she became rich, she wanted to help others. She created the Sarah Blakely Foundation. The foundation gives money away. A lot of the money goes to schools for girls. Blakely wants other women to have the same opportunities. She is happy to have money, but she is proud because she can give something to young women, so they can follow their dreams.

When people ask Blakely about her success, she talks about her father. Her father helped her become a strong woman. When she was growing up, he often asked her a question at dinner: "What did you fail at this week?" He thought failure was good because it meant she was trying something hard. Sarah learned valuable lessons from her failures. Then she turned those failures into success.

REFLECTION

1. In your opinion, what was the secret to Blakely's success?
2. How are you similar to or different from Blakely?

II

HEAVY WEATHER

Hurricanes are the biggest storms on earth, but they start small. They form in the Atlantic Ocean, and weather scientists watch them carefully. When a storm gets big and dangerous, it gets a name. These names are important because people start talking about hurricanes weeks before they arrive. They also talk about them for many years after they are gone.

The way we prepare for hurricanes and the stories we tell about them afterwards can teach us lessons. We learn about our neighbors and ourselves. Many of these lessons are positive. There are stories about people helping each other. However, there are also sad stories. Even when people know a hurricane is coming, they can still make mistakes.

3

BIG STORM COMING

Hurricane Ike was one of the worst hurricanes in history. The big storm came through the Gulf of Mexico and headed for Houston, Texas, one dark night in 2008. When it reached the shore, the wind was blowing more than 100 miles per hour (160 km), and the storm was hundreds of miles across. In a short period of time, it destroyed boats and houses, and it knocked down trees. Schools were closed, and many people lost electricity for weeks. I know because I was there.

My family and I live in Houston, Texas. My parents moved there many years ago, but my brother and I had never experienced a hurricane before. When Ike came, my brother Simon was twelve years old, and I was only nine, but I still remember almost everything about that hot September.

We first learned about the storm on the news. Then we talked about it at dinner. Our parents had to make a decision. Did they want to stay in the house, or leave the area? I My mother and I went to the neighbors to talk about it. I played with the cat while they discussed the situation. They talked for a long time, and they gave each other advice. After much discussion, they all decided to stay home. They called this "hunkering down." Hunkering down meant protecting the house and waiting for the storm to pass over.

After we decided to stay home, we prepared for the storm. We needed to make the house safe and get supplies. First, we cleaned the yard. My father did not want anything to hit the walls or windows when the wind started blowing. Sometimes he looked up at the tall trees over our house and shook his head. I liked the trees, but now they were scary. I hoped they would not fall on our house. I also worried about the squirrels. Many squirrels lived in the trees. What were they going to do when the winds came?

Twenty-four hours before the storm, we prepared inside the house. My mother cooked a lot of meat from our refrigerator. I filled water bottles, and Simon helped our father cover the windows with wood to protect the glass. I could hear them working. All the neighbors were covering their windows with wood, and the street was noisy.

After my father covered our windows, it got very dark inside. It was afternoon, but in the kitchen, it was like nighttime. After he put the last piece over the front door, we had to turn on the lights to see.

Later, my mom and I took some food to our neighbors. When we walked up to their house, she was surprised because they were not covering their windows. Instead, they were sitting in their kitchen, drinking coffee with friends. My mom got a cup of coffee and sat down with them.

"Aren't you covering your windows?" she said.

"Too much trouble," said Max. "It'll be fine."

Max had experienced several hurricanes, and he was not worried, so my mom said she wasn't either. That made me feel good. I wanted the storm to come. I was excited about it. My friend at school had told me that the trees might bend over and touch the ground.

My mom and I walked back to our house on the broken sidewalk. Under the sidewalk, the roots of the trees showed through the cracks. She looked up into their branches. "I hope they are still here tomorrow," she said.

Then she looked at me and stopped herself. "But it'll be fine. Our house is old and strong. It's survived plenty of hurricanes." I knew she was trying to make me feel better, so I smiled. We were at our yard now. Our little yellow house looked old and sad with wood over its windows.

Two squirrels ran up and down the tree by my bedroom window. Did the animals know that a big storm was coming? How about the birds? I watched several black birds fly across the gray sky. They called to each other. Were they giving a warning?

After dinner, my mom said felt nervous. She did not want to watch the weather on the news, so our family went outside again. We could walk in the middle of the street because no one was diving. Most of the houses had wood over their windows, so we could not see any lights. It was very quiet and peaceful, but the trees moved a little in a light wind.

"The calm before the storm," said my mom.

Back at home, our parents decided we should all sleep together in the middle bedroom because it had the most protection. We watched the news on the computer and learned that the storm was coming straight to Houston. There was no way to change our minds, but we felt safe, and I was tired, so I fell asleep quickly.

The next thing I remember was my dad waking me up. "Get up, Kat," he said. "You have to see this!" I opened my eyes. The wind was loud, and it was shaking the house. My dad had a light, and I followed him to the living room. He showed me a small space between the wooden boards. I stood on a chair and looked outside.

Through the rain, I could see the trees. Tall, strong trees were bending over. Their tops were almost touching the ground. I opened my eyes again. It seemed impossible for a tree to bend so far, but it did. My friend was right.

"Is it going to break?" I asked.

"No, it's not," said my dad. "That's what's so amazing. That tree can bend in a storm. It knows what to do!"

We sat and looked out in the rain and wind. Suddenly there was a noise, and the whole street was dark. That meant the electricity was gone. There was nothing more to see, so my father brought me back to bed.

In the morning, I woke up to the sound of rain. I didn't know what time it was because the house was dark and we could not turn on the lights. I ran to the window and looked out through the space in the wood. Everything was different. Our whole yard was full of broken tree branches. I could not see the grass or the street. It looked like an ocean of green. I opened the door and went outside to look.

It was raining a little, and the wind was still blowing gently. Many of the neighbors were coming outside. I could see their red and yellow raincoats. They gathered in the street to tell their stories: a tree fell on a house on the next street, but the people inside were not hurt. One man was taking care of some baby squirrels. I was happy to know that they were alive. Other neighbors were starting to clear the branches from the street. I really wanted to climb on the fallen tries, but my mom said no.

For the next two weeks, the city was shut down, so we stayed home. My friends and I got together every morning and played. At night, we went to someone's house for dinner because everyone was cooking food from their refrigerators. It was like one big party. I felt bad about the people that suffered from the storm, but I enjoyed that time, and I felt bit sad when the electricity came back on and we had to go back to school.

REFLECTION

1. Can you remember a storm from your childhood? What happened?
2. Do you think the family made a good decision? Why or why not?

4

LOST AT SEA

You are the captain of a ship, and a storm is coming. What do you do? You cannot stay near land. It is not safe for the ship. The storm will push the ship onto the rocks, and the ship will break apart. Instead, you must take the ship out to sea.

As you approach the storm, the sky becomes dark. The wind begins to blow. It creates waves. The waves get higher and higher until they are like mountains. You turn your ship to face a mountain of water. The floor seems to fall away as the front of your ship travels up the wave. You must hold on, or you will fall. You go up and up. Then your ship goes over the wave, and suddenly you are pointing down. You see the water coming towards you on the other side. The front of your ship goes under the water. You hold your breath.

This is the only way to survive the storm. If you turn to the side, and a wave hits you, it can turn your ship upside down. There is only one choice. You must point your ship straight into the next wave, and ride up and over. You do this again and again, and you hope that the front of the ship is strong enough to hold together until the storm ends.

The captain of the *Fantome* knew this. Guyam March grew up in the Caribbean, and he had a lot of experience on the Atlantic Ocean. He also knew about the risk of storms. Every year, hurricanes begin off the coast of Africa. They travel across the water, and they become powerful. When the wind reaches 75 miles per hour (120 km), these ocean storms become hurricanes. The winds blow in a big circle, sometimes hundreds of miles across. The size and strength of hurricanes make them very dangerous for ships.

However, Captain March knew something else. Hurricanes are not sudden. Scientists study the weather, and they can give information about storms. They can often predict the direction of a hurricane. Captains and ship owners can use this information to make decisions about safety. As a result, most ships escape from the worst storms. Captain March trusted this information when he prepared for a cruise in the fall of 1998. He expected the ship owners to watch the weather and make careful decisions about the safety of their ships.

The *Fantome* was a cruise ship, but it was not a regular cruise ship. It was old and beautiful, and it only carried about 100 passengers. These passengers paid a lot of money for a special experience. They ate excellent food on the ship, and they enjoyed swimming in the warm water.

The *Fantome*'s owners thought it was safe to start the cruise. Captain March welcomed the passengers on board, and the the *Fantome* set out the ocean. But then the captain heard some bad news. Hurricane Mitch was moving towards them. To be safe, the company decided to cancel the trip. Captain March let the passengers off in Central America. Then he talked to the ship's owners. The passengers were safe, but the ship was not. Where could the ship go, to stay away from the hurricane?

They had to make a difficult choice. The owner was worried about keeping the ship near land. The waves and wind might throw the *Fantome* against the land. The damage could be expensive, and it would be difficult to fix. The *Fantome* was one of the last tall ships, and it had historic value. The ship might even be destroyed.

Finally, Captain March and the owner decided to take the *Fantome* back out into the ocean. They thought they could keep the ship safe by hiding behind an island. The island could protect them from the big waves.

Mitch was not an ordinary storm, however. Mitch got stronger and stronger. Wind speeds increased to 180 miles per hour (290 km). Some winds got as high as 200 miles per hour (322 km). The waves were as high as a four-story building. Then the news got worse. Mitch was coming straight to the island. The *Fantome* was trapped.

Some ships can try to get to the "clean side" of a hurricane. The clean side is the back of the storm, and the waves are not as strong there. The front of the hurricane is called the "dirty side." It is very dangerous. The *Fantome* tried to get to the clean side, but it could not escape, and it got caught in the worst part of the hurricane.

Captain March did his best to steer the *Fantome* up and over the waves, but he had more bad luck. The storm stopped moving. The ship was in the middle of the wind and waves, and it had no way to escape. The captain and a few of his men continued to battle the storm for several hours. Then the ship lost radio connection with people on land.

No one knows what happened. There were no survivors to tell the story. A few life jackets washed up on a beach. Then someone found a lifeboat. Experts believe that the ship went down quickly. Maybe water got into it. Maybe it rolled upside down. Maybe it broke apart. They only know that the *Fantome* and all the people on board were lost.

The sad story of the *Fantome* is a lesson about the power of nature. People can hope a hurricane will go in a different direction. They can say, "Maybe it won't come here." But no one can change the direction of a storm. Hurricane Mitch did not stop with the *Fantome*. It continued towards Central America. When it reached Honduras, it destroyed hundreds of thousands of homes and killed tens of thousands more people. Weather scientists named Mitch the second deadliest hurricane in two hundred years.

Today, ship captains remember the *Fantome*. They hope that when the next storm comes, they can make a better decision, or at least have better luck.

REFLECTION

1. Was the *Fantome* disaster bad luck or bad decisions?
2. When was the last time you changed plans because of dangerous weather?

III

STREET SMART

What do you think when you hear the word *stranger*? When you search for it online, and you click on images, you might see scary people. Usually, it is nighttime on a dark street. Maybe someone is looking out a window. She is afraid. This is one way people think about strangers.

However, there is also another way to think about strangers. In English, some people say, "A stranger is a friend I haven't met yet." They like to meet new people.

One thing is usually true about strangers, however. When you meet one, interesting things can happen. You might have an adventure. You might learn something new. Maybe you will face danger. Maybe you'll have a chance to help another person. When you travel, a meeting with a stranger can be important because you can learn something from them, and you can teach them something too. You can connect with a different person, and you can learn about a different kind of life.

5

IS TALKING TO STRANGERS A BAD IDEA?

You are riding on an airplane. You take your seat by a window, and a man sits next to you. He is your age. What do you want to happen? Do you hope he puts on headphones and leaves you alone, or do you want him to talk to you? How will you feel if he looks at you and says, "So are you traveling for work or for fun?" In the first situation, you are free. You can read or watch movies. In the second you are in a conversation, and it might continue for an hour or more.

Interestingly, most people prefer the conversation. They feel good when they talk to a stranger. Psychology researchers have studied people on airplanes and busses. They asked different groups of people to talk to another passenger or stay quiet. Afterwards, they asked people how they felt about the experience. The people who talked to strangers were happier.

So, if you are like most people, you choose the conversation. You tell the other passenger about your trip. You might share information about your plans, and get or give advice.

Perhaps it will be useful for you, or maybe you will hear a good story, but your connection with this person will generally leave you in a good mood.

This research suggests that people are interested in each other. It explains why people often choose to visit public places. For example, people with big comfortable kitchens still go out to eat. They stand in line for an expensive cup of coffee at Starbucks. The real reason is not the coffee. They simply want to sit at a table near other people.

At the same time, people have mixed feelings about strangers. People often feel afraid when they are alone on the street, especially at night. Parents teach their children not to talk to strangers. A lot of ordinary people cannot relax with someone who dresses differently or speaks differently.

Why do some people feel comfortable with strangers, and others do not? Here is an explanation. Talking to strangers is a skill. Some people do not have much experience. They do not know how to start a conversation or change the topic. Maybe they are afraid because they cannot end the conversation easily.

Other people feel okay with strangers because they have confidence. They enjoy listening. They know how to control the conversation. Take the airplane situation, for example. Maybe you enjoyed learning about the other traveler for a little while, but now you are ready to read your book. What can you do? With a friend, you can be informal and say, "Okay, I'd like to read now."

With a stranger, people are generally more formal, so you want to be polite. You might spend some extra time slowing down the conversation. You can speak less and create silence. Then you can say something about your book. Or you can leave your seat, and when you come back, pick up your book and then say, "This is such an interesting book. I want to finish it before we land."

Psychologists say people should not be afraid to talk to strangers. Having conversations with new people is not just for airplanes and bus rides. There are many experiences when talking to a stranger is important. Successful business people and other professionals use conversational skills to meet new people in their work, at parties, or at other social occasions.

The psychologist Amy Morin has written a book called *13 Things Mentally Strong People Don't Do*, and she helps people develop skills for talking to strangers. According to Morin, the first step may be the hardest: starting a conversation. People often think others do not want to talk to them, so they do not start conversations. In fact, many people want to meet other people, but they hope the other person will talk first. Once you know this, she says, it can give you confidence. The important thing is to practice.

When you start, do not ask strangers personal questions. This can make them uncomfortable. Pick something in the environment. This technique explains why so many people talk about the weather. It is something everyone experiences, but it is not personal or political. Here are some examples of places where strangers can talk to each other.

Dog walkers in the neighborhood can be a good place to practice. A dog makes a good topic of conversation, and someone with a dog is usually not in a hurry. People like their pets, so you can compliment the dog. Ask a couple of questions about their pet. Then say, "Enjoy your walk." The experience should be positive for you, the dog owner, and maybe even the dog.

Take the skill to the next level by giving someone a compliment at a party. Women do this more than men. They might say something nice about another guest's jewelry or shoes. Often jewelry has a story. Maybe a necklace was a gift from a relative. Maybe it belonged to her grandmother. Often the speaker will give another compliment in return.

Men often start conversations by talking about sports. A man in a bar will comment about a game on the television screen: "Jones is off his game," he says. The next guy will agree or disagree, and the conversation continues. The game gives them a focus, but it is not too personal. When they share ideas about the game, they feel closer.

Once you get to know people a little, try to be curious. Curious people are often skillful at talking to strangers. They do not feel nervous because they want to learn. They might offer to help tourists, and they share useful information.

Finally, many social people are good at recognizing nonverbal information. They watch someone's eyes or the way they move, and they understand how the person is feeling. They can tell when a person wants to keep talking or end the conversation. They use that information to make decisions about whether to talk, listen, or end the conversation. "I had better let you go," is an example of a polite way to say good-bye.

The most skillful people often live in cities. Talking to strangers is a part of their daily life, and lots of practice helps. These people can reach out to a waiter, a taxi driver, or someone in line at the store, so they are never really alone.

REFLECTION

1. Are you good at talking to strangers? Would you like to be better at it?
2. What might stop you from talking to a stranger?

6

THE GIRL ON THE BUS

The morning light woke Maria, but she did not open her eyes immediately. Many thoughts and feeling came to her mind. First, she felt sick. Then she felt happy because she remembered why she felt sick: she and Juan were going to have a baby. Morning sickness was normal. She was pregnant, and she needed to eat something. Finally, she felt nervous because today was her doctor's appointment.

Maria took a breath and opened her eyes. She listened to her family starting the day. Her husband Juan was in the next room. He was talking on the phone. She put her feet on the ground and stood up. She was dizzy, but she was okay. She went to the kitchen where Mama was cooking breakfast.

Juan ended his call and gave Maria a quick kiss. "Good morning, beautiful," he said, and he smiled at her. Then his face changed. "I have some bad news. I have to go to work today."

"But what about the doctor's appointment?"

"I'm sorry, sweetheart. This customer is important. He's the guy who buys and sells cars, and he needs me."

"And you need him. I know." Maria looked at her eggs. "I can go by myself. I'll take the bus."

Her mother sat down at the table with them. "I'll go with you."

"No, Mama," Maria replied. "You can't walk. You need to stay here! I'll be fine."

"Are you sure?" Juan asked. "Are you feeling okay? We can change the appointment to a different day."

"It's a bus ride," Maria laughed. "I'm not crossing a desert."

An hour later, Juan dropped Maria off at the 71 bus stop. She found a seat near the front and watched as the bus filled with workers. They were reading their phones, and a young man with headphones was singing. Maria leaned against the window. She was still a little sick, so she tried to focus on baby names. *Esmeralda if she's a girl*, Maria thought, *and Rafael if he is a boy*. Maria liked long names. Besides, they could use short names like Esme and Rafi.

The bus moved off the freeway and into the medical center. She could see doctors in white coats on the sidewalks. She liked doctors. They always seemed so confident.

Maria got off the bus and walked to her appointment. She was early, so she looked at a magazine while she waited. She knew a little English, but she couldn't understand all the words. A famous person was also pregnant. There was a photo of her with a big round belly on the beach. Maria did not know the woman's name, but the big belly was a little scary. Maria had started seeing pregnant women every-where, and she could not imagine being so big and needing new clothes. She was still small and wearing her own dresses.

Dr. Hernandez came out to greet Maria. Maria felt

comfortable with her, and during the appointment, they talked.

"What do you think, Maria? A boy or a girl?" said the doctor.

"I can't decide. Can I have one of each?" Maria joked.

"Maybe next time," the doctor said, and smiled. "There's only one heart beat." Listen.

Maria smiled at the sound of her baby's heart. It was loud and strong.

After the appointment, Maria walked out into the hot sun to wait for the bus. A few people were sitting, so she had to stand, but the bus came quickly. She got on and found a window seat in the back. She leaned against the glass. She was thirsty, too, but she would be home soon. The bus was comfortable, and she closed her eyes.

Suddenly, Maria woke up. She sat up and looked out the window. The bus was in a strange place. She did not recognize the street or the buildings. There were stores and gas stations, but there were no sidewalks. The bus was outside the city. Maria had missed her stop.

Maria suddenly felt afraid. She reached beside her to get her phone. But there was nothing there. She looked around. Where was her bag? It was not on the seat. She looked under the seat. No bag. No bag meant no money and no phone. Someone had stolen everything while she was sleeping.

Maria's fear increased. She looked around. An old man was sleeping across from her, and there were two women at the front. The bus stopped, and the women got off.

Maria got up and walked to the front of the bus. She wanted to talk to the driver, but he looked angry. He swung the bus around a corner and into a neighborhood with houses. A sign said, "Shady Village."

Maria was afraid to leave the main street, so she rang the bell and got off. But as soon as she stepped into the sun, she realized her mistake. She did not have any money or a phone, and it was very hot outside. She thought about the fruit her mother had packed for her. It was still in her bag.

Maria started walking. Maybe she could get help on the main street.

A car slowed down next to her, and Maria turned. Two women and a man were in the car. One woman said, "Are you okay?" and something else in English that Maria did not understand. Maria did not trust them, so she said, "No, thank you," and kept walking.

Back on the main street, Maria found a bus stop back to the city. She had no money, but she tried to figure out the English words in her head. "Someone took my bag!" she practiced to herself. She wanted the bus to come fast. She needed water. The baby needed water.

An older woman joined her. "Oh, my goodness, it's hot," said the woman.

Maria nodded.

"Such a day!" the woman repeated. Then she looked at Maria. "You don't look too good, child. Are you pregnant?"

Maria understood, and she nodded again.

"I can tell, you know. I had eight of them myself." The women spoke slowly, and Maria tried to follow her words. She thought that the woman said she had many boys and maybe one girl, but she was not sure.

Finally, the bus came, but it was not her number. It was a 260. But Maria could not stay in the sun. She got on, and she said her sentence carefully. "Can I ride the bus? Some-one… they took my purse."

The bus driver was a young man, and he was wearing dark glasses, so Maria could not see his eyes. She waited. He made a noise. Then he said, "Yeah, right." Maria felt her face get hot, but she did not want to go out in the sun, so she waited.

Finally, he nodded his head towards the back of the bus, to show Maria she could get on.

Maria took a few steps and sat down. It was cooler now, but she needed to get water soon. The woman from the bus stop sat behind her.

"I heard that. I understand. Are you okay? Do you know where to go?"

"Maybe," she said. Her voice showed that she wasn't sure, though.

"Do you speak English?"

Maria shook her head, "No, a little."

"I'm Myrtle," said the woman, carefully.

"Maria."

After a few stops, Myrtle asked Maria to get off the bus with her. "It's okay. I'll get you a phone, dear."

Maria looked outside. She still did not know where she was, but she trusted Myrtle. She followed Myrtle off the bus. Myrtle went into a building. It said YMCA on the side. Myrtle took Maria's hand and helped her into the building. It was a gym. There were many people in exercise clothes, and Maria could hear balls hitting the floor.

Myrtle brought Maria to the desk, and spoke to someone in English. A young woman with dark hair looked at Maria. Then she went away and came back with a bottle of water. She gave it to Maria.

Gratefully, Maria took the bottle and drank. The water was cold, so she had to drink slowly, but immediately she felt better. The woman pointed at a chair and told her to wait. Maria sat. She drank some more water.

The woman went away and came back with a young

man. He sat down and said to her in Spanish, "My name is Rafael, and I can help you. Do you need to call someone?"

Rafael gave Maria his cell phone, and she called Juan. He sounded worried, "Maria! Where are you? I was so worried. Baby, are you okay? Where are you?"

"Let me explain!" Maria started laughing. It was so good to hear his voice. She gave the phone to Rafael so he could tell Juan the address. Then she started to get up. She wanted to find Myrtle and thank her.

"Where is Myrtle?" she asked Rafael. "I want to thank her."

Rafael pointed to Myrtle, who was walking slowly down the hall. Maria hurried after her. "Thank you!" she said.

Myrtle smiled and said something in English. Maria looked at Rafael for help.

"She says not to worry," said Rafael. "It is an honor to be needed."

REFLECTION

1. Have you ever helped a stranger? For example, a tourist who needed directions?
2. What does Myrtle mean when she says, "It is an honor to be needed"?

IV

HOUSE PET NATION

Americans spend over 60 billion dollars a year on their pets. This surprising number shows that people in the U.S. love their animals. Many think of their pet as a member of the family. In fact, they give human names to their dogs and cats. In the past, a dog might be named Spot because there was a spot on his face Now his owners might call him *George* or *Mary*, which are names of kings and queens.

Pets now have doctors, clothes, and special toys. There are special dog parks so dogs can run around and play with each other, and cats get special furniture. Some people take their pets on vacation and make sure the animals have entertainment. The importance of pets is an interesting new social development. Clearly, these pet owners are getting something special from their animals, but what?

7

WHAT DO DOGS THINK ABOUT PEOPLE?

A few years ago, cute dogs were big business. Pet owners wanted pretty puppies with big eyes. Dog breeders are people who raise and sell dogs. These breeders mixed different dogs to create attractive dogs. They could sell these dogs for a lot of money. However, now the market is different. Fashionable people want a smart dog or a dog with a loving personality. But what does that mean? How do you know a dog is smart or kind?

This new interest in dogs' personalities has become important. Now, some people take their pets to universities for testing. Pet dogs are research subjects in a new academic field called "canine cognition." *Canine* means "dog", and *cognition* means "thinking." Canine cognition experts study dogs' brains.

One of these academic programs is at Yale University. It is part of their psychology department. The researchers want to answer several questions: How do dogs think about their environment? How do dogs solve problems? And how do dogs make decisions?

Dog researchers developed a test to find out how dogs feel about their owners. First the researchers train the dogs to sit still. Then they put each dog in a machine. The machine measures the dog's brain. Then they give the dog two smells. First, the dog smells a stranger. In most cases, the dog's brain stays the same. Next the dog smells its owner. When this happens, the machine lights up the happiness part of the dog's brain. In other words, the dog is happy when it smells its owner, but it does not feel happy when it smells strangers.

Researchers found more physical evidence of love between humans and dogs. When pet owners and their dogs played together, they produced a chemical in their bodies. It is the same chemical that parents produce when they hold their babies. Owners feel love when they look into their pet's eyes, and researchers believe the pet feels the same.

These studies show dogs care about their owners and want to make them happy. This has an effect on owners. They like knowing that their pets actually love them. Because of this knowledge, owners try harder to communicate with their pets.

Many dogs can learn to understand some human language. For example, a famous dog named Chaser knows more than a thousand words. When her owner says the name of a toy, Chaser can find it in a large pile of toys. This means the dog understands some vocabulary. The owner can also tell Chaser to pick up the toy. This means the dog understands some grammar.

Another dog, Trevor, showed the ability to solve a problem. Trevor got separated from his owners on a trip to the country. While the family was traveling, they made several stops to rest. But at the end of the day, when the owners stopped at a park, they noticed Trevor was gone. They were worried. They drove back to all the places places they stopped at before, but they could not find Trevor. They gave up, and they went back to the park.

Sadly, the family crossed the road and walked a short distance to the picnic area. Many people were sitting at tables, enjoying their lunch. Suddenly, the family saw Trevor. He was sitting by a table, waiting for them. He had a look in his eyes that said, "What took you so long?"

Trevor's past experiences at picnics helped him predict the right place to go. When he got separated from his family, he used his nose to go through the parking lot and find the picnic tables. Then he waited. He did not go into the trees or down the road. He knew that his family often sat at picnic tables, so he just found the table and waited.

While smart dogs like Trevor are good in many ways, dog experts also give a warning. Smart dogs often cause trouble. A dog with high intelligence gets bored easily, and a bored dog can learn to open doors, steal food, and eat shoes or destroy furniture. As a result, there is a new way to spend money on pets: people can buy special toys for smart dogs. The dog must solve a problem to get some food, for example.

Some dog owners solve this problem by taking their animals to special day care centers. The dog day care center is like a school. Human workers entertain the dogs with games and activities. They write reports about the dog to give to the owners. In fact, many of them do not use the word "owner." Instead, they have a new word. They call them "dog parents." This change in human/dog relation-ships surprises some people who are not animal lovers, but others say it just shows how smart dogs really are.

REFLECTION

1. What do you think about calling dog owners "dog parents"?
2. Do you know any stories about dogs?

8

THE DANGEROUS DESIRE FOR
DESIGNER CATS

Cats are important to humans. They are pets, and sometimes they have jobs. One job is to catch rats and mice. Another job is to a make people laugh. Some people make a a lot of money creating funny cat videos and selling the videos to Internet companies. However, the most valuable cats are simply beautiful.

In recent years, cat breeders found a way to raise prices for cats. They started mixing ordinary house cats with wild cats. These designer cats look like tigers or other wild cats, and cat lovers pay a lot of money for them. However, many wildlife experts think mixing wild and pet breeds is a bad idea. But cat lovers do not care. They love their cats, and they will pay a lot of money for them.

Two of the most popular designer cats are Bengals and Savannahs. A Bengal is an Asian wild cat mixed with a house pet. It is bigger than a regular cat. The Bengal has black spots on its gold fur. It also has stripes, so it looks like a small tiger. Bengals with green eyes are more expensive. A beautiful Bengal can cost between $1000 and $10,000.

The Savannah cat is a mix of an African hunting cat

called a Serval and a house cat. A Savannah has smaller spots, longer legs, and bigger ears than a Bengal. It looks fast, wild, and elegant. The price can be high. Some people have paid $25,000 for a beautiful Savannah cat.

One breeder, LifeStyle Pets, created an even more expensive cat. This cat was called an Ashera. Asheras were very beautiful. They had green eyes and a gold coat with black spots. Tall, thin, and proud, they were animal celebrities. LifeStyle Pets said the Ashera was a special new breed. One Ashera had a price of $125,000.

However, there was one problem with the Asheras. They looked like Savannahs. In fact, they looked *a lot* like Savannahs. When a Savannah breeder recognized his cats in the Ashera advertising, he told reporters. He said LifeStyle Pets was selling Savannahs with a new name. After that, Asheras disappeared from the market, but the story proved something interesting. Some people will pay a lot of money for a good-looking cat.

The news about the Ashera also caused a lot of discussions. Many cat breeders were upset. They thought LifeStyle Pets did something wrong. They also worried about the attention. They did not want the public to ask questions about wild mixes. The breeders needed wild cats from Africa and Asia to create Bengals, Savannahs, and other new cats. They did not want people to worry about the dangers of having wild cats in their communities.

Owning wild cats has now become a social issue. On one hand, the government must protect the animals. Wild cats need a clean place to live, healthy food, and space for exercise. On the other hand, the government must protect people. Wild cats are natural hunters, and they are bigger then regular cats, so they can be dangerous. Many breeders do not have experience or knowledge of wild cats. When a wild cat escapes, it can kill other pets or even hurt people. When people are in danger, and the police may have to kill the animals.

In 2011, a terrible thing happened in an Ohio community. Ohio allows wild animals as pets, and one man had a private zoo. He kept many African animals, including 35 wild cats. One day, the man opened all the cages and let the animals go. The animals ran out into the community. It was getting dark, and the police had to protect people in the area. They began shooting the animals. By morning, all the wild cats were dead.

Groups such as Big Cat Rescue and many animal rights organizations use these stories to warn people about dangers. They say wild cats should not live with people. A worker from Big Cat Rescue in Tampa, Florida, says a wild breed looks cute when it is young, but it changes when it becomes an adult. Because of its wild blood, it is unhappy in small spaces, and it can become dangerous. He says cat owners often call him to take their pet away after it grows up.

Breeders disagree. They say the pets are friendly, and their customers are happy. This is at least partly true. At a chatroom for Savannah owners, people describe their pets as friendly and fun. The cats sleep with them, play with their children, and sit by the door to welcome them when they come home. One woman says her cat is very nice to her four-year-old daughter. She completely trusts the animal.

Humans and cats have lived together for thousands of years, and beautiful cats appear in art and literature. It may be dangerous to bring a gold and black, green-eyed, half-wild cat into their home, but some people want it. Their cat is like a beautiful piece of jewelry.

There could be another reason too. The beautiful

Savannah who walks around the apartment, playing with a toy or stretching her legs in the morning sunlight, represents the wild. Even a person living in a city apartment can have a connection to nature. The danger and beauty are all part of the attraction.

REFLECTION

1. What is your experience with cats?
2. Should breeders have the right to sell half-wild designer cats?

V

DESIGNING FOR DISABILITY

"Special needs" is a term that describes people with disabilities. Maybe they cannot walk, cannot hear, or cannot see. Some special needs people have different ways of thinking. In the past, people with special needs were often separated from other people. They went to special schools, and they did not have the same opportunities as others.

Now all that is changing. Many people are recognizing the value of *all* people, and they use descriptions like "differently abled" (People without disabilities are "able-bodied."). To help differently abled people participate in society, many designers are creating technology and buildings for this population.

9

ANYONE CAN SKI

The ski area is busy with spring skiers. Many of them are taking a break at the bottom of the mountain. They get hot drinks or meet a friend. One of the skiers calls out to a young man. "Hug," she says. "I want a hug!" He is confused, but the smile on her face is real. He gives the smiling woman a hug. "Now a high five!" she says.

The woman's name is Donna, and Donna explains that she is feeling happy. She came down the mountain four times. For most people this is easy, but not for Donna. Donna is a skier with special needs. It is hard for her to control her body. Volunteer skiers help her, so she can have fun skiing down the mountain just like everybody else.

Here at Winter Park in the mountains of Colorado, other skiers with disabilities have a similar experience. Some of them cannot walk, and others cannot see, but with the support of the National Sports Center for the Disabled (NSCD), they have a team of professionals and volunteers. These helpers adapt technology, train families, and ski with the people with disabilities to keep them safe.

"The NSCD makes sure that everyone has a chance to go on the mountain," explains Diane Eustace, Marketing Director for the organization. "We sit down with the skiers and talk about their goals. Then we create a program for them." Sometimes the program involves physical and mental support, as in Donna's case. Other times, the organization provides special equipment.

One popular solution is the "sit ski." Some people cannot walk because of a disease or an accident, but they can still use their arms. Engineers have created a special chair on skis. The chair protects the skier's legs, and the skier holds special skis with her hands. The skier does not have to use her legs because she can use her hands to turn. The unique design gives these skiers control and confidence. They cannot walk, but they can ski.

Another device looks like a bicycle on skis. It is for people who can use their legs a little. They can sit on the bike and turn with their hands. The center also has slider skis for skiers who need a little extra balance. Eustace describes a young woman named Katy Leasure. Leasure's disease makes her weak, but she enjoys skiing. Leasure skis with a bike ski. Her family members also love to ski, and they are happy that they can enjoy the sport together.

NSCD does not just provide equipment, however. They help in many ways. When a person is using special equipment, there is always a professional or volunteer with them. The volunteer is also a skier. He helps the skier go up the mountain, and he is there when the person falls.

"Some skiers need a lot of help because falling is not okay," says Peter Sherman, a volunteer with NSCD. "They can get hurt more easily, but it is important for them to have experiences like everyone else."

When somebody asks if it is stressful to be responsible for a skier with a disability, Sherman shakes his head. He prefers to focus on success. He talks about the challenges for the skiers, and says he learns from them. "The skiers are our inspiration," he says. Many volunteers come back every year. "Some volunteers have been doing this for 25 years. I am going to do this for 25 years!"

The volunteers get a lot of training before they are matched with a skier. There are about 25 paid instructors and about 800 volunteers at Winter Park, explains Eustace. The professional ski instructors have two jobs. They teach the disabled people how to ski, and they teach family members and volunteers. At first, the volunteers follow the instructor and watch. Then the helpers experience the disability equipment themselves. For example, they might try sit skiing, so another helper can practice skills. In this step by step process, the volunteers become confident.

Some volunteers ski with blind people. The volunteer becomes the eyes for the skier. The first time a blind person tries skiing, it can be difficult. The instructor uses a rope to guide the skier. However, after the skier develops some skills, the instructor or a volunteer skis next to the person and gives directions. "Turn left here; turn right; slow down." The skier and the volunteer work closely together. Little by little, they make progress, and the skier improves.

Like most people, athletes with disabilities enjoy challenges. Many of them enter competitions, and Winter Park is a good place to train. Tyler Carter is a Paralympic athlete who participated in the Sochi Olympics in Russia. The Paralympics is just like the Olympics, but it is for athletes with disabilities. When Carter first walks into a room, it is difficult to see his disability. The 24-year-old skier is tall and strong, but inside his right ski boot is a prosthetic leg. This means Carter learned to ski with one real foot and one artificial foot.

Carter loves competition, and he is training for the next Paralympics. But he also cares about helping other people with disabilities. He understands the lessons that people with disabilities can teach to able-bodied people. Some people have disabilities we can see, but others have problems we cannot see. "Everyone has something going on," he says, "It's all about adapting. We adapt to overcome whatever challenges or obstacles we face."

Carter is proud that athletes with disabilities ski on the same hills as other Olympic athletes. There might be small changes, but most of the race is the same. The main difference is that the Paralympic athletes have bigger challenges. And their challenges are all different. The organization uses a special system of points so that more abled skiers have fewer points, and less abled people get more points.

"It's not a perfect system," he says, "but it works."

Carter and other athletes like him are helping to change people's ideas about disability. Paralympics athletes get media coverage and a big audience. They train with professionals at places like Winter Park, and they give hope to families and other people with challenges. They also inspire engineers and others to invent new technology for sports and daily activities. Most of all, they teach that having a disability does not mean a person like Katy Leasure must sit in front of the television. She and her family can go out in the world and live a full life.

REFLECTION

1. Do you know someone with a disability? What have you learned from the person?
2. What changes have you noticed in how people think about disability?

10

DESIGN FOR THE DEAF

When Georgette Brand tells a joke at lunch, she needs a lot of space to talk. Georgette is deaf, so she needs to use her hands to communicate. She cannot tell a good joke if she does not have space. Her friends need to see both her face and her hands to understand the joke. This is just one thing that designers think about when they design a school for the deaf.

Georgette hopes to go to Gallaudet University. Gallaudet is a special university for deaf people. The school has a long history of adapting its campus for the deaf. The university was built in 1864, and the designers wanted to make life comfortable for people who use their eyes but not their ears. For example, they created a special doorbell. When someone pushed the doorbell, it did not make a noise. Instead, a weight dropped on the floor, and people could feel it. Then they knew a visitor was at the door.

The doorbell was a unique invention and an example of design for the deaf. Today designers continue to support the needs of deaf people, but now they have more technology.

Gallaudet's doorbell is now a flashing light. There is a lot of glass, so people can see through walls. There are not as many stairs or sharp corners, so students can walk and talk easily. They do not have to take their eyes away from their friends.

To create these details, designers learn about deaf culture and needs. Many of them are hearing people, so they spend time with deaf and hard-of-hearing people and talk to them. Deaf people in North America have a language called American Sign Language, or ASL. ASL has a special vocabulary and a grammar. There are jokes, poems, and funny expressions. People who use ASL are proud of the language and their identity. At Gallaudet and in deaf culture, being deaf is a way of life.

When a hearing person communicates with a deaf person, they sometimes use an interpreter. The interpreter knows both languages, so she can translate. To be polite, hearing people speak directly to the deaf person and not the interpreter. The deaf person might not hear the words, but he can see the speaker's face and expressions. Then he will look at the interpreter for a translation, give his answer in sign language, and the interpreter will translate.

As designers listen to students and learn more about the deaf community, they use their creativity to make special classrooms. In a traditional classroom, desks are in rows. But this does not work for deaf students. They need to see each other, so the desks are in a circle. Designers also paint the walls in dark colors, so students can see each other's hands.

These new designs for the classroom were successful, so the university created a new kind of architecture. It is called Deafspace. This design recognizes the needs of deaf people, and not only at Gallaudet. In fact, according to the National

Institute on Deafness, two to three children out of every 1000 is born deaf or hard of hearing. The number is even higher for adults. Deafspace design can help make work places and homes more comfortable for this population.

The changes have made Gallaudet more convenient and student-friendly, but another type of technology is more controversial. A medical device called a cochlear implant (CI) can help deaf children hear. While it allows deaf children to grow up in a hearing world, the device often separates these children from the deaf world.

When deaf children get CIs, they may not learn ASL, and they may not have opportunities to join deaf communities. They can hear, so they attend schools with hearing people. If they have hearing parents, they can experience their parents' world. Of course many of them do join deaf communities, but this percentage is lower than the general deaf and hard-of-hearing population.

Many deaf people are upset about CIs because they believe that deaf children do not need a "cure" for deafness. They want hearing parents to understand their feelings before they separate children from their deaf identity.

Because of the controversy, parents must make difficult decisions. On the one hand, society and organizations like Deafspace help deaf people function in the hearing world. On the other hand, medical devices can give people a choice about joining deaf culture.

Georgette's parents decided to give her cochlear implants so she could have that choice. Now she lives in both worlds. Sometimes she talks to her hearing family, and other times she uses sign language with her deaf and hard-of-hearing friends. She is happy that she knows ASL even though she can hear and speak English. "I would not be me without it," she says.

REFLECTION

1. What do you think is important for hearing people to know about deaf culture?
2. What do you think about cochlear implants?

VI

OTHER EARTHS

Humans love to explore. Now technology is giving us opportunities to learn about other planets. Already, humans have walked on the moon and sent robots to Mars. These robots sent back interesting information. We now know that Mars has water, and maybe in the past, our neighboring planet had life. What does that mean?

We depend on scientists to study space and give us facts. However, scientists are not the only ones exploring the possibilities of space. Artists are also curious, and they help us imagine those worlds. In books, movies, and other art forms, artists may help us to imagine life on another planet. Then we can decide if we want to look for it.

11

WHERE IS PROXIMA CENTAURI?

Fifty years ago, most people thought space was a cold, empty place. Today scientific discoveries are changing our understanding. The universe may have millions of planets. These planets circle distant suns. Some of those planets could have land, water, and air. In other words, there may be other earths.

The study of space started with telescopes. About 500 years ago, people discovered that special glass could make things look bigger and closer. They started using this early technology to look at the stars. Now we can see the stars with powerful modern telescopes.

To work well, a telescope needs darkness and thin air. Many telescopes are in space or in deserts. Some of the strongest telescopes are in the Atacama Desert in Chile. This mountain desert is the driest place on earth, so it is a good place to study the night sky. Scientists here can study the stars and look for planets.

To find a planet, researchers look for small changes in the light from a star. When a planet crosses in front of the star, it makes a small shadow. Scientists measure the shadow and measure its distance from its star. Some planets are far away from their suns, so their water is ice. Other planets are close to the sun. Those planets are too hot for water. A planet in the middle is like Earth. It has the right temperature for oceans, lakes, and rivers. When a planet is at this distance, it is in the habitable zone.

Researchers like to find planets in the habitable zone because they might be similar to earth. They might have air like our earth, and they might have life like our life. Nobody has found life on another planet yet, but some people are looking.

Our closest neighbor planet is Mars. It is in the habitable zone, and we have already sent robots there. These robots use solar power from the sun. They move around on the Martian desert, take pictures, and do experiments. Then they send information back to earth. Because of these experiments, scientists now believe that Mars has water. There is ice underground, and it melts during the Martian summer. If Mars and Earth have water, it is possible that other planets have water too.

In addition to research on Mars, scientists look for planets around other stars. In 2009, a group of researchers found a possible planet near a star they named Gliese 581. They measured the planet's distance from its star. It was in the habitable zone. Some researchers thought there was more than one planet. People became excited about the planet, but there were problems. Other organizations did not find the same information, and after a few years, many scientists agreed that Gliese 581g was a mistake. The planet did not exist.

The news about Gliese 581g was disappointing, but it still had a positive effect. People became interested in looking for habitable planets. Since then, scientists have discovered hundreds of possible planets in habitable zones. In fact, the universe is full of planets. Only some of the planets are the right distance for life, but there could be millions of them.

Unfortunately, these planets are hundreds and some-times thousands of light years away. (A *light year* is the distance that light travels in one year.) We cannot travel to them, and any life on these planet cannot travel to Earth.

Then in 2016, scientists made a new discovery. The European Southern Observatory in the Atacama Desert found a planet. This planet was circling a weak orange star called Proxima Centauri. The Centauri planet is in the habitable zone, and it is closer to Earth than other planets. This earth-like planet is still 4.25 light years away, but engi-neers and astronomers say it is close enough for a visit. The technology for traveling at the speed of light does not exist yet, but scientific organizations are looking for a way.

A program called Starshot is developing special tech-nology for high-speed space exploration. Starshot is an international group of business people and scientists. The group wants to look for habitable planets. Their very small spacecraft will travel at one fifth of the speed of light. The spacecraft is too small to see, but it can arrive on Proxima Centauri in less than twenty years. Also, scientists can send a thousand of these tiny spacecraft. Some might not arrive at Proxima Centauri, but others might.

After the first visit, researchers will send larger robots. These robots will be similar to the robots on Mars, but they can send more information about a planet. At the same time, human visits to Mars can help solve some of the prob-lems of space travel. For example, scientists can look for new sources of energy for powering space ships.

It is difficult to predict what the first visitors might find on the Proxima Centauri, but we know it will be different from Earth. The planet is bigger than our Earth. Also, one side is always day, and the other side is always night. The light never changes, so visitors will never see a sunrise or a sunset. The colors are different, too. Everything will look orange. A year will be 11 days.

Then there is the big question: does Proxima Centauri have life already? Does it have forests, fish, birds, and creatures, like on our own Earth? If so, what do they look like? Could they have language? Technology? Art? And most important of all, are they friendly?

REFLECTION

1. Do you think humans will travel to another planet in your lifetime? Should we?
2. Imagine there is intelligent life on the planet of Proxima Centauri. Do you think they would want to visit Earth? Why or why not?

12

HOW ARTISTS PREDICT THE FUTURE

In the 1860s, a French writer named Jules Verne became famous for his imagination. Verne wrote about an underwater ship called a submarine. It had windows, electric lights, a kitchen, a dining room, and even music. The submarine stayed under the ocean, and it never came to the surface.

Verne's book was called *20,000 Leagues Under the Sea*. In the book, the captain of the submarine does not like people, so he stays deep in the ocean. He explores the undersea world and discovers strange creatures. The book became very popular for its dark story but also because readers could imagine life in a submarine.

Because of Jules Verne, people felt like they were experiencing a possible future. There were submarines at the time, but they were very small and simple. In his novel, Verne gave people a chance to dream about a day when submarines had more technology and were more comfortable. People could believe in the possibility because someone had already described it.

Verne's prediction came true. Today we have

submarines that have electricity and can travel deep in the ocean for weeks at a time. Most are owned by the military, but many are used in exploration. In 2012, for example, the filmmaker James Cameron went to the deepest part of the ocean, the Mariana Trench, in a submarine called *Challenger Deep*. He was safe and comfortable inside a small ship that went seven miles below the surface. When he did this, Cameron turned Jules Verne's imaginary science into a reality.

Verne did not stop at the ocean. He also imagined space travel, and he used the technology of the time to make a prediction. In a novel titled *From Earth to the Moon*, he described a trip to the moon. In the story, people used a giant gun to shoot a rocket to the moon. People rode in the rocket and landed on the moon. Later, a fellow Frenchman named Georges Méliès filmed *From Earth to the Moon* with actors on a stage. In the film, the explorers find plants and strange creatures. They start a war with Moon people and then return to Earth.

Sixty-seven years after the film came out, three astronauts went to the moon. Their spacecraft rode a rocket into space. They circled the moon, and then one man stayed in the main spacecraft. The other two men got into a smaller spacecraft and landed on the moon's surface. The astronauts, Neil Armstrong and Buzz Aldrin, were the first humans to walk on the moon. Their experience was very different from Verne's imagination. They found a cold, gray desert with no plants and no creatures, but Verne's imagination had become reality.

The imagination of Jules Verne shows a relationship between art, science, and society.

Artists like Verne look at new information or technology and ask themselves, "What does this mean? How will people use this technology?" Then they use their creativity to answer those questions with stories. People read and discuss the stories, and they imagine the future. In this way, science fiction storytellers can inspire young people to become scientists and explorers.

Today, many filmmakers are following Verne's example with movies about space. In the movie *Gravity*, audiences watch humans swim through the air. In *The Martian*, they watch a scientist grow food on Mars. In *Interstellar*, three astronauts search for new planets. Interestingly, the details about planets and space come from scientific facts. The filmmakers want their movies to seem as real as possible.

No one knows what other planets are really like, but these movies feel real. After people watch them, they may think about projects in space. They might want to support the international space station or maybe continue the search for life in the universe. They can easily imagine their children visiting these planets because they have seen them on movie screens.

Although we have no information about life in space, there are also artists who imagine humans meeting aliens from other worlds. Many of these meetings are friendly. In *E.T.*, a small, lost creature gets trapped on Earth, and some children help him go back to his planet. In *Arrival*, the filmmakers imagine learning an alien language.

Other meetings explore possible problems. In *Avatar*, tall, blue, human-like creatures have a close relationship with nature. When humans arrive with their technology, looking for resources, they threaten the aliens. In contrast, the space creatures in *Alien* are big, ugly, and angry. They hate humans and want to kill them.

Writers, filmmakers, and other artists cannot see the future. They have never been to space, but these creative people help us explore different possibilities. They give us hope, warn us of danger, and remind us that the first step to achieving anything is to imagine it first.

REFLECTION

1. Describe a science fiction character (from a film or book) that shaped your view of science and technology.
2. What do you expect to happen during the first meeting between humans and aliens? Where did your ideas come from?

ADDITIONAL BOOKS FROM WAYZGOOSE PRESS

Wayzgoose Press publishes a variety of books for students of English, including self-study guides, textbooks, more volumes in the *Big Ideas* reader series, and other series of graded readers. Find our full range of titles on our web page at

http://wayzgoosepress.com

To be notified about the release of new titles and special contests, events, and sales from Wayzgoose Press, please sign up for our mailing list, which you can do from the website. We send email infrequently, and you can easily unsubscribe at any time.

Made in the USA
Columbia, SC
21 February 2023